A Little Prince in the Land of the Mullahs

The true story of a teenager who stood up to the Mullahs' regime in Iran.

Ahmad Raouf Basharidoust

1964—1988

Foreword: Linda Chavez

Preface: Ingrid Betancourt

Biography: Massoumeh Raouf *Basharidoust*

Scenario: Summer Harman

Research: Summer Harman, Massoumeh Raouf *Basharidoust*

Art work: Bunga, David Fernando Monroy Mallorca

This book has been translated into French, German and Farsi and will later be translated into other languages.

A Little Prince in the Land of Mullahs; The true story of a teenager who stood up to the mullahs' regime in Iran

Copyright © National Council of Resistance of Iran – U.S. Representative Office, 2019.

All rights reserved. No part of this monograph may be used or reproduced in any manner whatsoever without written permission except in the case of brief quotations embodied in articles or reviews.

First published in 2019 by
National Council of Resistance of Iran - U.S. Representative Office (NCRI-US),
1747 Pennsylvania Ave., NW, Suite 1125, Washington, DC 20006

ISBN-10 (hard cover): 1-944942-30-0
ISBN-13 (hard cover): 978-1-944942-30-4

ISBN-10 (paperback): 1-944942-29-7
ISBN-13 (paperback): 978-1-944942-29-8

ISBN-10 (e-book): 1-944942-31-9
ISBN-13 (e-book): 978-1-944942-31-1

Library of Congress Control Number: 2019941838

Library of Congress Cataloging-in-Publication Data

National Council of Resistance of Iran - U.S. Representative Office.
A Little Prince in the Land of Mullahs
1. Iran. 2. Human rights. 3. Massacre. 4. Middle East. 5. United Nations

First Edition: June 2019
Printed in the United States of America

These materials are being distributed by the National Council of Resistance of Iran-U.S. Representative Office. Additional information is on file with the Department of Justice, Washington, D.C.

Every great change will come only when you embrace the hero in yourself; give up what is most dear to you and do what seems most difficult

Our hero's story continues...

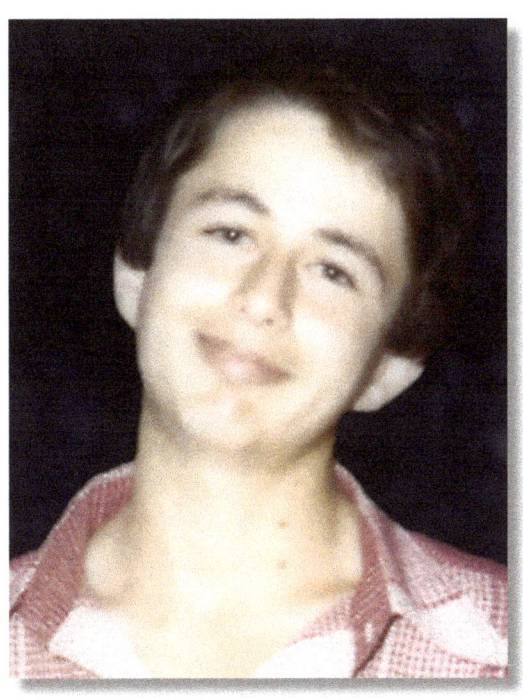

Ahmad Raouf Basharidoust
1964—1988

Foreword

A Little Prince in the Land of the Mullahs revives the little hero in the reader by telling the story of a brave young man who wants nothing more than to live the life that all boys and girls want: to be free, happy, and secure in his homeland. Unfortunately, the boy comes of age after the Ayatollah Khomeini has transformed Iran into a nightmare. The Ayatollah and his clerical followers enforce rules that make life impossible for any freedom-loving people. The Ayatollah does not allow free speech or freedom for people to gather and meet as they choose. The country, with a great history and civilization, becomes poor, with free and equal access to education denied to women and the clerics controlling what may be taught to everyone.

The hero of this story is an ordinary boy with an extraordinary heart and courage. He cannot watch idly as his family, his community, and his country are torn apart. He decides he will fight for what he believes. Thus he, like many youths of his generation, joins the leading opposition movement, the Mujahedin-e Khalq, but the mullahs will not allow such dissent. Like tens of thousands of others, the little prince suffers. He faces arrest, torture, and ultimately sacrifices his life.

This is the story of 30,000 Iranians, the majority of them under age 30, who could not stand by and do nothing. They paid with their lives, but they serve as an inspiration to all of us. Unfortunately, the slaughter of the innocents by Ayatollah Khomeini and his regime in 1988 did not stop 30 years ago, but goes on to this day. The men who replaced Khomeini are every bit as blood-thirsty and dangerous as the Ayatollah was. But most people do not know of this terrible atrocity. We must all be vigilant to make sure that the sacrifices of those like the little prince are not repeated without notice today.

Linda Chavez

Linda Lou Chavez was formerly a White House director of public liaison, Staff Director of the U.S. Commission on Civil Rights, was elected by the United Nations Human Rights Commission to serve a four-year term as U.S. Expert to the U.N. Sub-commission on the Prevention of Discrimination and Protection of Minorities.

Preface

Ahmad's story, told in comic book form, is certainly not a children's story.

Yet, that is how her sister Massoumeh wanted to share it with us. Perhaps that is because this story, which she has carried in her heart for 30 years, is made up of images that are too strong - those of her own life - images that are painfully engraved and that she did not want to betray.

Massoumeh did not want to write just another story to talk about her brother. She did not want to present cold statistics and a politically correct analysis. Massoumeh wants us to grasp with our emotions that which is inaccessible through reason.

She needs to bring her brother back to life, so we can get to know him, so he can enter our space, our time, and also - who knows - maybe finally our hearts.

Telling the story of your little brother is a need, of course, but it is above all a right. It must honor Ahmad's heroism, the majesty of his spirit, his beauty, his charisma. That is why she draws him for us and makes him speak, because she knows that he alone can be his best spokesperson.

At the turn of each page we discover him in action, surrounded by his family, in his house, in his street, in his school, with the beautiful landscapes of his native country as a backdrop. We meet his friends and with them, his dreams and fears. Ahmad is there, in front of us, playful, intelligent, courageous, and poetic. We see him growing up in the tumultuous Iran of the 1980s. He became an adult, almost in spite of himself, probably too early, shaken by the violence of Khomeini's dictatorial regime in Iran.

From Ahmad's hand we are entering the heart of the Iranian Resistance — that of the People's Mojahedin. Early on in his twenties, he and his companions dream of a better future, without oppression, without fanaticism, without exclusion.

And in this suffocating and misogynistic world of the mullahs, his heroes are his mother and sister: a sister who manages to escape from prison, a mother who dies under the persecution of the regime's executioners.

The story of the little prince in the land of the mullahs reveals to us, without any pretenses, the human tragedy facing millions of Iranians. With Ahmad, we can go through this tragedy, live it and try to understand why, so that the truth can no longer be hidden, so that justice can be done, and so that the liberation so long awaited by the Iranian people can happen.

Ingrid Betancourt

Ingrid Betancourt, a Colombian-French politician, became a Senator in 1998 in Columbia. In 2002, while a candidate for the presidential election, she was kidnapped by FARC, and held hostage in Colombian jungle until rescued in 2008. Upon her release she continued her fight against human rights violations around the world and became an advocate for those who suffer and do not have a voice.

Find the hero in you

Hello, world!

I suppose once in a while, everyone loves to live out an adventure or mystery. To follow in the footsteps of Heroes and make a difference in the world.

My story carries a message that will inspire the Hero in you.

For decades, my story and message was buried by dark forces... Through these pages, by your reading my story, I am Reborn.

Darkness will only prevail when there is no Will to keep Hope alive.

Join me. Hear my story and help me keep Hope alive on these dark streets of life.

Spread the message and inspire others...

      You WILL make a difference.

CHAPTER 1

HELLO WORLD ..HERE I COME !

Yep! I was loved, as you can see! But soon I would learn that life was a BIG trial... And that it is up to me to face those trials and transform from who I am to who I long to be.

They said I was a handful— I can now see myself at 2.
I was always a warrior. A warrior is a hunter— he aims/calculates/acts.
No one can push him around or decide his fate for him. A warrior will take time to observe and study, and only then leap for his goal.

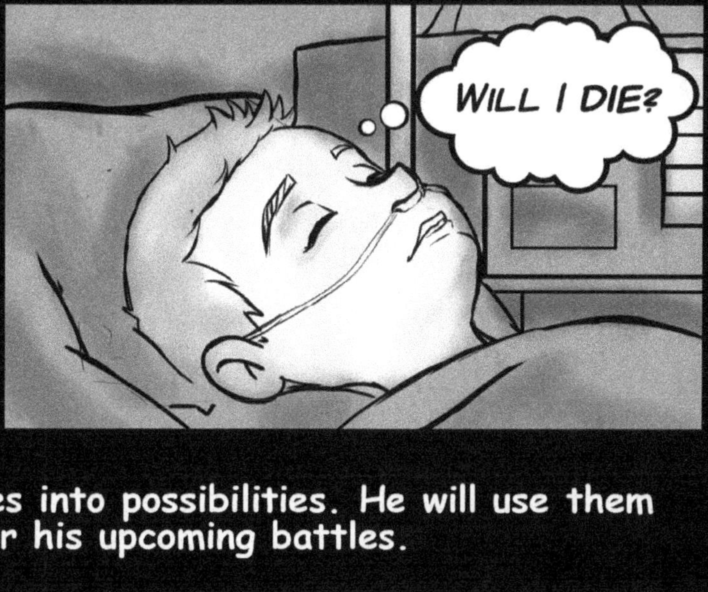

Age 8- Iranian New Year, Nowruz was coming and we were sent to our uncle's in Tehran along with our grandma.

Although we had much fun, we really missed our mom. She stayed behind in Rasht.

AHMAD, LITTLE BRO—
WE ARE GONNA HAVE US SOME FUN!
WOW! FINALLY, SOME FUN!

LOOK! WE CAN SEE MOM FROM HERE! DON'T BE SAD
MOM, I MISS YOU SO MUCH
COME ON, GUYS! WE ALREADY ATE OUR KEBABS. YOURS ARE GETTING COLD.

NO, NO, STOP! PLEASE DON'T TAKE HIM!
I WISH MOM WAS HERE
AAAAAA NO, NO! PLEASE!

NO, NO! PLEASE!
WHAT THE—?!
SHHHHH LEAVE IT! IT'S SAVAK!! TAKING SOMEONE

POOR MOM. I CAN'T IMAGINE WHAT SHE IS GOING THROUGH NOW

Until that night, I'd never believed monsters were real, and could be the guy next door. The Savak were the Shah's notorious secret police.

I later learned that anyone could be a Savak member. They were not to be trusted.

They were teaching us that life would be easier if you don't concern yourself with issues you don't understand- in other words: you should submit to fate and circumstances around you. Well I didn't really agree with that, & since we didn't have the Internet, Twitter, SMS or Facebook, I had to ask dad.

CHAPTER 2

Finding a spark

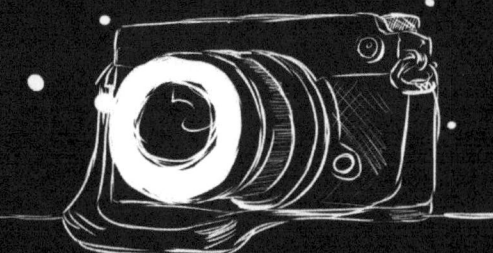

My world, my choice- Iranian New Year Nowruz March 1978
I learned that there are three kinds of people in this world: Those who make things happen; those who talk and watch things happen; and those who will do the unthinkable to stop bad things from happening.
It didn't take long for me to choose my group.

Panel 1:
- WE GOT A NEW CAR.
- HERE SHE GOES AGAIN!
- YES AND THIS WAS HOW I MANAGED TO TRANSFER MYSELF TO RASHT
- TOO CLEVER, DEAR
- HAPPY NOWROOZ, AHMAD!
- THANKS, BROTHER
- GROWING UP ISN'T SO FUN!

Panel 2:
- AHMAD, BE HAPPY
- COME ON, AHMAD. TIME FOR JOY!
- CLAP CLAP
- COME AND JOIN ME!
- UNCLE!!! THAT'S EMBARRASSING! NO WAY!!

Panel 3:
- I THINK WE NEED A MIRACLE TO BRING CHANGE
- THE LAST WE HEARD OF HIM WAS BEFORE THE ATTACK ON THE UNIVERSITY.
- YEAH...
- EH?!!

Panel 4:
- WHAT'S WRONG WITH OUR COUSIN?
- HER SISTER WAS PICKED UP BY S**** (SAVAK)
- THEY FOUND SOME BOOKS

Panel 5:
- SO WHAT?? WILL BOOKS BRING DOWN A SYSTEM? WILL THEY?
- NO! BUT PEOPLE DO! NOW HUSH!!

Panel 6:
- WHY?? WE'RE AT HOME!!
- YES-BUT WE DON'T WANT TROUBLE... WALLS HAVE MICE AND MICE HAVE EARS, SO SHUSHH!
- HOW CAN WE SEE A WRONGDOING AND DO NOTHING! THIS WORLD NEEDS HEROES AND CHANGE.

AND... CHANGE WAS UNDERWAY.

OVER THE NEXT SIX MONTHS, A NEW IRAN BEGAN TAKING SHAPE.

- Protests in two major cities, Tabriz and Isfahan were crushed.

- The newspapers went on strike, which led to a general strike of the Bazaar, and on October 21, 1978, the crippling strike of the country's oil industry occurred.

- October 1978: The Shah asked French president Giscard d'Estaing to give protection and safe haven to Khomeini, who by then was exiled from Baghdad to Kuwait.

- November 6, 1978: General Gholam Reza Azhari, a general of the Armed Forces, was appointed as the prime minister. He enforced martial law to curb the unrest.

- December 11, 1978: Eleven million peaceful protestors demonstrated, demanding change in response to General Azhari's statement that called protests a hoax, claiming they were using audiotapes to trick people into believing that protests were on the way.

EVENTS LEADING TO THE 1979 REVOLUTION

- January 4-7, 1979: The Guadeloupe Conference was held by the UK, France, USA and West Germany. Discussions included politics in Iran.

- January 4, 1979: Bazargan was appointed Prime Minister of the interim government by Khomeini.

- January 8, 1979: President Giscard d'Estaing of France transferred confidential message from US President Jimmy Carter, regarding policy to avert "revolution" in Iran, to Khomeini.

- January 16, 1979: The last set of political prisoners was released from the Shah's prisons by the people, including my idol, Massoud Rajavi.

- January 19, 1979: The Shah left Iran.

- February 1, 1979: After several years of exile, Khomeini were flown back to Iran from Paris.

- The people challenged the army loyal to the Shah by chanting "disarm." Khomeini, he imposed himself as a Imam, rejected the call and continued with behind the scenes deals revealed in the public media later.

- Protesters faced live bullets and were killed..

As the battle continued on the streets, another was simmering in each of us.

A decision whether to quit in the face of danger or to push even harder and never surrender.

One thing was clear:

Death comes in many forms – but worse than death is when a person remains silent in the face of injustice.

**February 11, 1979
The Final Shift**

An ocean of blood and hope for a new Iran.

The regime collapses. It is a triumph for the Revolution. The Pahlavi dynasty ends and a new era begins.

Millions rejoice on the streets, celebrating the happiness they created.

WHAT A SIGHT!

YES HAJI... CHANGE THE F***** PICTURE!

COME ON, LET'S GO TO THE FRONT!!!

* In the jargon of the fundamentalists they call a respected elderly « Haji ».

CHAPTER 3

New Month, New Change

The aftermath of the 1979 Revolution was the dawn of knowledge, but knowledge without a purpose is like a car without a steering wheel.

It can lead you over the cliff.

And me?

Well, I was on the hunt for a purpose.

So we read and debated a whole suitcase of books we had bought from the street for a week.

"Your life starts when you take control of your fate."

Cyrus the Great

THE NEW CHANGES IN IRAN WERE THE BEGINNING OF AN END – THE HARD-GAINED "FREEDOM" WAS BECOMING IMPOSSIBLE TO KEEP.

- February 18, 1979: Khomeini founded the "Islamic Republic Party" (his own party) and created local paramilitary forces (The Bassij), to gain control over the citizenry.

- February 23, 1979: Massoud Rajavi, leader of the PMOI (the People's Mojahedin Organization of Iran), publicly expressed concern over several events, asking for full and equal participation by all sectors of society in decision-making, with no exceptions.

- March 3, 1979: Offices of political groups, including that of the PMOI, were attacked by Iranian Hezbollah.

- March 10, 1979: Thousands of women participated in a protest against "forced hijab," and were supported by progressive political groups such as the PMOI.

- March 18, 1979: Kurdish protests were suppressed in northwest Iran.

- March 23, 1979: A peaceful protest by the ethnic Turkmen minority was violently suppressed.

- March 31, 1979: National referendum to make Iran an "Islamic Republic" was held. People were asked to either vote YES or NO, with no option other than to vote for an Islamic state.

- April 14, 1979: The sons of Khomeini's popular rival, Ayatollah Taleghani, who supported a moderate Islam, were arrested. Protests in response to this arrest were reported in newspapers.

THE SOCIETY WAS DRIFTING APART OVER "DEMOCRACY" AFTER ONLY A COUPLE OF MONTHS.

THE NATIONAL REFERENDUM THAT SET IRAN'S COURSE AS AN "ISLAMIC REPUBLIC" WAS MASSIVELY RIGGED.
IT WAS FOLLOWED BY A NEW ROUND OF ARRESTS, INCLUDING MOHAMMAD REZA SAADATI, A PROMINENT FORMER POLITICAL PRISONER AND A MEMBER OF PMOI.

- Khomeini publicly lashed out against groups that spoke for democracy and called them the Enemy of Islam.

- August 3, 1979: The Assembly of Experts (mainly mullahs who supported Khomeini) was appointed to supervise changes.

- August 14, 1979: Aggressive attacks were carried out against the PMOI offices.

- August 17, 1979: In a televised broadcast, Khomeini said he should have hanged people in public from the start in order to prevent rising opposition.

- August 18, 1979: Swift military suppression of the people of Kurdistan was ordered by Khomeini.

- August 20, 1979: The official newspaper, Kayhan, reported that 22 newspapers had been shut down.

- December 2, 1979: A national referendum was held for the so-called new Islamic constitution. The pro-democracy PMOI did not take part and announced the drafted constitution failed to protect basic fundamental rights for all groups, ethnic and religious minorities, and women. In return, they announced their Platform for Freedom & Democracy.

CHAPTER 4

Finding the hero in me!

January 20, 1980: We had been very successful in spreading the word! A famous saying goes: Democracy and Freedom are never served on a silver platter... And to gain these, you must first lose everything... They will bloom when we protect their seeds with wisdom, perseverance and galant bravery.

They say every great change will come only when you embrace the hero in yourself give up what is most dear to you and do what seems most difficult.
The next day at high school, my chance had come.

That day, I won again! ABAZARI was a paid thug - a member of the *local guards.
They beat the daylights our of us, yes, but they NEVER conquered our will, not did they deter me.
* The "Pasdaran" are the "revolutionary guards corps" established for suppression in Iran.

BY THE END OF JUNE 1980, IT BECAME CLEAR THAT OUR GOALS HAD BEEN REALISTIC, AND WE HAD DONE THE IMPOSSIBLE, PREVENTING THE COMPLETE FAILURE OF THE 1979 REVOLUTION FOR FREEDOM AND DEMOCRACY. DESPITE ALL THE TRICKS AND CHEATS, AND ATTACKS AGAINST EVERYTHING WE HAD, SOME PROGRESSIVE CANDIDATES WERE ACTUALLY ELECTED. HOWEVER THEY WERE PREVENTED FROM ENTERING THE ASSEMBLY.

- April 1980: A series of provocative speeches by Khomeini aired on TV, asking the Iraqi people to rise and rid themselves of "tyrants." He started a feud with the neighbouring country, Iraq, to distract attention from Iran's real fight for democracy and silence dissenting voices.

- April 18, 1980: Violent attacks on universities by pro-Khomeini thugs and the Revolutionary Guards left 16 dead and 208 seriously wounded. A total of 500 sites and places were attacked under the pretext of "cultural revolution." It was known that the university was the main stronghold of progressive groups and intellectuals.

- June 12, 1980: PMOI held its convention of 200,000 people in Tehran's AMJADIEH stadium on the subject of "What is to be done?" It was violently attacked by organized thugs.

- June 25, 1980: Khomeini strikes back at the PMOI, naming them "worse than infidels" and forcing the closure of all their offices. Then Khomeini began a new front: The IRAN-IRAQ WAR.

- September 22, 1980: The beginning of the Iran-Iraq War.

September 10, 1980: Our first Street exhibition. We had worked hard for it.

CHAPTER 5

June 20, 1981 - The turning point

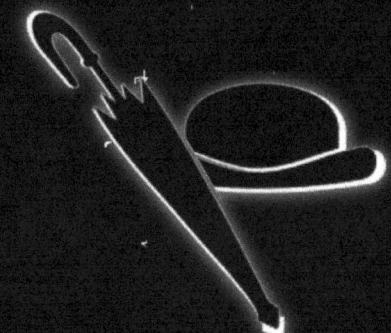

The Turning Point – June 20, 1981: RASHT, IRAN

TO PROTECT THE INNOCENT... TILL FREEDOM DAWNS

NO KIDDING?! WE EACH HAVE CHOSEN WILLINGLY. SO DON'T PLAY WITH US!

GUYS- IT'S NOT TOO LATE...ANYONE WHO WANTS TO WITHDRAW, STILL CAN-

ARE YOU KIDDING US OR DO YOU DOUBT OUR DEVOTION?

AGREED

YEP...

SORRY GUYS, IT'S JUST THAT WE ALL MUST GO WITH FREE WILL... FLYERS FOR THE PROTEST

WE MUST TRY OUR LAST SHOT AT PEACEFUL PROTESTS. LET'S SEE HOW THE EXTREMISTS TOLERATE IT!

TEHRAN

Later that day..

Tear gas- but the people dug in and threw paper to help us make fire.

KILL THEM WHERE YOU SEE THEM!!

Ettelaat newspaper reported unidentified teenagers executed.

..And the Guards opened fire... Thugs were mostly guided by MULLAHS, including some prominent figures such as Ghaffari.

That day, in all major cities, people showed support for FREEDOM through organized, disciplined, and peaceful protest. In Tehran 500,000 took part. Then, Khomeini issued a fatwa that gave his Revolutionary Guards and thugs permission to kill on sight. Later they blame us for all the killing. I remember a prosecutor told one of my friends who had been tortured, that he had tortured himself and was blaming the Guard.

...many disappeared

Worse than infidels" –That day, I felt the sky was bleeding red in sorrow for all the innocent protesters killed. It wasn't safe to go home, so I tried to keep a low profile in a nearby ruin, which was a secret play spot with my sister.

The car stopped after a while.
I listened intently, unable to see anything.

MAMA!!! MAMA!!!

POOR KID! HE MUST HAVE BEEN WITH HIS MOM WHEN SHE WAS CAUGHT...

TAKE THIS ONE TO HAJI...

WHAT IS THIS PLACE? I CAN'T SEE THROUGH THIS BLINDFOLD, NOR SPEAK THROUGH MY GAG

THE FLOORS ARE SLIPPERY! OOOPH! WHAT IS THAT STENCH? IS THAT BLOOD?

MAMA!!! MAMA!!!

AAAH DARLING...

I was taken, blindfolded, to a room... and that's when it started.

STAY BRAVE!

WHERE DID YOU MEET? WE KNOW YOU BOMBED THE OFFICE...

WE ARE SOFT ON YOU BUT THEN THIS WON'T LAST

TALK, YOU F****** OR YOU'LL GET A TASTE OF OUR HOSPITALITY!!

YOU'RE A FEISTY ONE, EH?! TAKE THIS!

MIGHTY GENEROUS OF YOU. TAKE MY BLINDFOLD OFF SO I CAN SEE MY HOSTS! IS THIS ANY WAY TO TREAT A GUEST?

YOU AND THE REST WILL EITHER ROT HERE OR IF YOU'RE LUCKY, YOU'LL DIE SOON!

I WILL F****** YOUR MOM BEFORE I FINISH WITH YOU

THE IMAM HAS DECLARED WE CAN KILL YOU, RAT.

NO USE TRYING TO RESIST, LITTLE BOY...

MOSAYEB!! HE IS THE TEAM LEADER

BRING THE WET LASH.. WE'LL TAKE TURNS. THE BIGGEST PIECE LEFT OF YOU WILL BE YOUR FINGER. WE'LL GIVE YOU THE SPECIAL!, RAT!

NO NAMES, YOU IDIOT!

I passed out at around 300 lashes.......
I won't go into the gruesome details.

May 1982: AFSARAN Prison

NAAH!

YOU OK, KID? YOU CERTAINLY GOT THEIR ATTENTION! MY BOY, BUT KINDA STUPID...

GOD! THE PAIN!

THEY TOOK 60 INMATES FROM A WARD AND JUST TWO CAME BACK ALIVE. IT WAS A COUP DE GRACE FOR 58 MEN, MANY MOJAHIDIN AND SOME MARXISTS.

HUH!?

IT'S MY 6TH INTERROGATION. THEY ONLY KEEP YOU ALIVE FOR TWO REASONS, FOR INFO OR TO BETRAY YOUR FRIENDS. SO... I'D SUGGEST YOU DON'T PLAY THE HERO

LISTEN CAREFULLY! NO BRAVE ACTS, KEEP A LOW PROFILE

WHY DON'T WE HAVE BLINDFOLDS?

THEY MUST NOT KNOW ME. OTHERWISE, THEY'D USE MY SISTER FOR TORTURE, TOO. SO.. THEY STILL DON'T KNOW WHO I AM... GOOD - YES! LOW PROFILE

YOU'RE PAST THE BLINDFOLD STAGE. IT'S NOT TOO LATE: LOW PROFILE.

AHHHH MY LEGS!

IN SOME S*** HOLE OF THE GUARDS

YOU MUST TEND TO YOUR WOUNDS— AS YOU CAN SEE, TWO OTHERS HAVE GIVEN UP THEIR SPACE FOR YOU

LET HIM BE, WE MUST HELP HIM ADAPT

THERE ARE 12 OF US IN A 2-BY-3-METER CELL. WE MUST WORK AS A TEAM!

YOU'LL GET THEM BACK...

CAN'T FEEL MY LEGS...

THANK YOU!

NICE TO MEET YOU. HEY, YOU ALL LOOK LIKE MUHAMMAD ALI— AFTER A BIG FIGHT!!

HA!! I SEE YOU'VE STILL GOT SPIRIT!

WE NEED A BIT OF SPIRIT HERE!

WELCOME BRO!

WHAT'S HAPPENING? WHERE ARE THE REST? ARE THEY SAFE? OH - GOD - PLEASE DON'T LET ANYTHING HAPPEN TO THEM. SAVE MY TEAM - TAKE ME INSTEAD. PLEASE... HERE IT IS - I'VE GOT TO GET THROUGH THIS— GOD! HELP ME STAY STRONG

THIS IS IT! THIS IS WHEN I RELY ON ALL MY LOVE FOR OUR PEOPLE...

WHO ARE THESE GUYS? CAN THEY BE TRUSTED? WHAT'S NEXT?

In those first few hours, despite my exhaustion and scrambled mind, my first goal was to have control over the situation

CHAPTER 6

FIRE

June 1982: Officers' Club Prison (AFSARAN), RASHT.

MAKING A RADIO WITH BREAD CRUMBS. YOU GUYS SAID YOU WANTED A RADIO, RIGHT? HAHA, JUST JOKING!

WHAT ARE YOU DOING NOW, AHMAD?

THIS IS WHAT I CALL ART!!

YEAH, SOMEONE TELL THE LOUVRE WE HAVE ANOTHER MICHELANGELO

HA HA! WE SHOULD DO AN EXHIBITION WITH HIS TALENT!

COME AND GET IT!

LET ME GUESS... KAFOUR RICE WITH POACHED LICE EGGS!

HEY, HYPOCRITE RAT!! YOU GOT A VISITOR!

NOW WHAT?

??!!

HE'S NO RAT!

AGREED.. MORE LIKE A SWALLOW.. FREE!

BRAVE ONE

MY DARLING LITTLE BOY

MOM!?

MY LITTLE PRINCE. YOUR SISTER ESCAPED PRISON TWO MONTHS AGO. THEY STILL CAN'T FIND HER. SHE WAS HERE TOO- IT'S TWO MONTHS NOW

I COULDN'T COME EARLIER- THEY WOULDN'T ALLOW IT

OH MOM! HOW FRAIL YOU LOOK- IF ONLY YOU KNEW HOW MUCH I LOVE YOU

THANK GOD! THANK GOD- TELL HER I'M SO PROUD OF HER. SHE MUST CONTINUE WHAT WE LEFT UNFINISHED!

MY DARLING BOY. IF ONLY YOU KNEW ABOUT THE ATTACKS ON OUR HOUSE AND HOW MUCH I WAS TORTURED AFTER THAT- BUT NO - NEVER WILL I TELL YOU. MY DARLING FRAIL BOY, MY BRAVE LITTLE PRINCE. FIGHT! FIGHT!

MOM, PROMISE YOU'LL BE SAFE- AND DON'T GIVE UP. BRING US NEWS FROM THE OUTSIDE - TRY TO GET IN TOUCH WITH THE RESISTANCE

MY BRAVE AHMAD, YOU TAKE CARE. MAY GOD BLESS YOU. I'M SO PROUD OF YOU - YES- YES. NEXT TIME..

Our paths crossed only once again. Later, I was again tortured, and she came to visit me! I will never forget her brave and determined face. She passed away after a lengthy battle with cancer

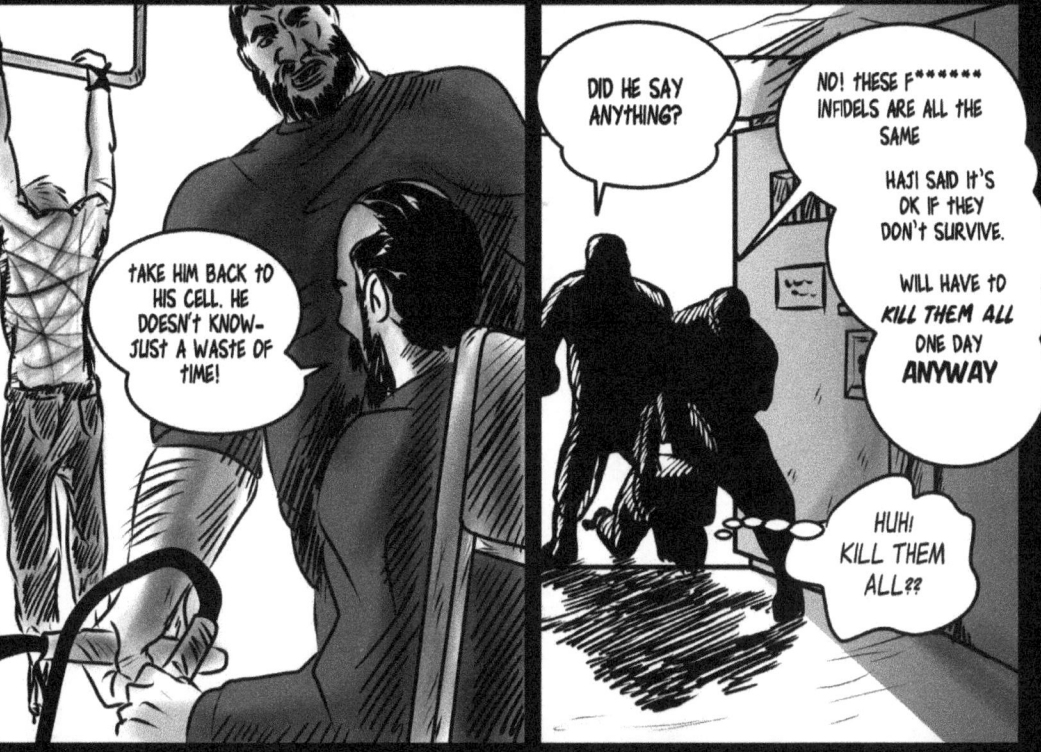

Back in our cell - Strange though it may seem, with my wonderful friends who were like family, it was like being home. They took care of me until I was stronger.

After a few weeks, I could join them in handball- a great distraction that raised our spirits and took our minds off our ordeals in that dungeon. The two Motaghi brothers- Rashid and Reza- had made a ball out of socks. I was the youngest of them all!

The fire spread, choking us with smoke. We were running out of oxygen. Some tried to boost morale by joking or singing anthems, but the situation was grim.
We were a strange combination of prisoners.
There were those who could not continue and had caved in to the tyrants (we called them quitters), along with Marxists- and progressive Muslims all in one ward.
ONLY TOGETHER COULD WE FIND A WAY TO SURVIVE.

A couple of days later I woke up in a hospital room, chained to my bed.

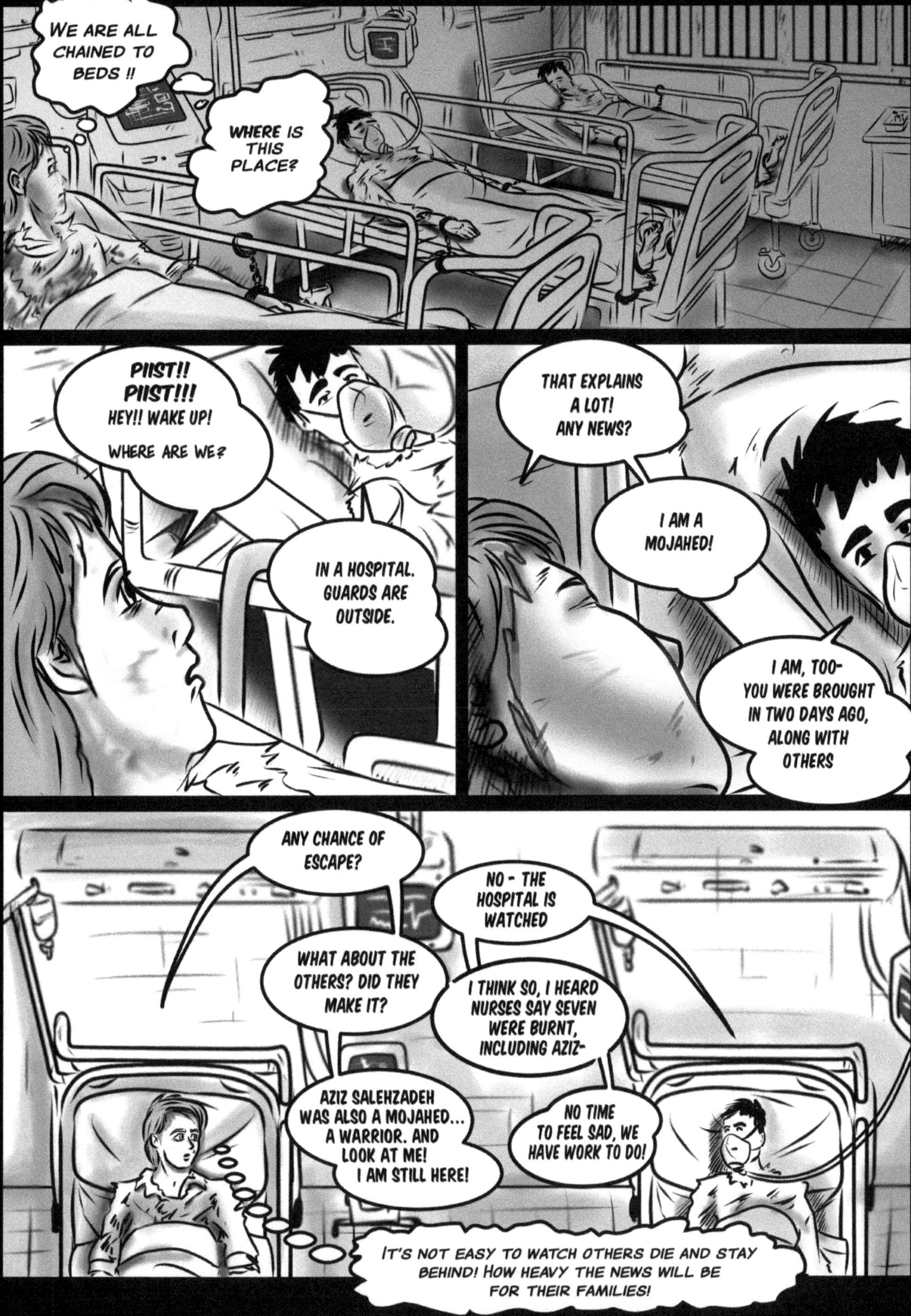

March 21, 1983: Persian New Year's Day (one week later) -
After the deliberate arson by the guards, we were transferred to SEPAH prison near Pol Aragh in Rasht. There, we decided to commemorate and honor of our fallen inmates by showing our collective determination.

LEAVE IT. WE'LL JUST GET A GOOD BEATING!!

HOW'S AHMAD?

NO- WE MUST PAY RESPECT TO THEM

YES! WE SHOULD!

I'M FINE... WE MUST PAY TRIBUTE IN MEMORY OF THOSE FALLEN IN THE FIRE!

HOW? HOW DO WE DO THAT?

YES GUYS, WE SHOULD

CLAP CLAP
CLAP CLAP
CLAP CLAP

LONG LIVE FREEDOM!! HAIL TO ALL HEROES LOST ON THE ROAD TO FREEDOM...

HEY!! WHAT??

HUH??

OOHOOH I DON'T FEEL WELL

WHAT'S WRONG MOHAMAD-ALI?

IT'S OK, AHMAD. JUST FEELING A LITTLE FAINT

GUYS, SOMEONE CALL THE GUARDS. HE MUST GO TO THE CLINIC!

THEY WON'T DO A THING!

WE'LL **MAKE** THEM...

GUARDS!! GUARDS!! A SICK PRISONER NEEDS TO GO TO THE HOSPITAL. I'LL BANG THIS DOOR ALL DAY UNTIL YOU DO SOMETHING!

WHAT THE FU***** DO YOU WANT, HYPOCRITE?!

YOU TAKE CARE

AHMAD, THANK YOU....

We won at last. He was taken to the hospital and we later learned that he managed to escape and join the Resistance.

CHAPTER 7

MORSE CODE & MY MOM

TICK--
TICK--
TICK--
TICK--
SOS

He was right: we paid a heavy price for it. When forced to choose between life and integrity... A warrior will choose integrity. Giving and loving and caring for others are the greatest riches a human can know. When lost, we also lose our humanity.

In GOHARDASHT, there were three main groups of prisoners: Those who would stand by their friends and defend humanity against the devil; those who broke down and sold their souls to the devil; and those who stood on the sidelines for their own protection.

Winter 1987: I was transferred to RASHT prison and released in 1988. That day was a unique and solemn day... I was met by my family outside the prison... MOM was absent.

I Was Free, but I had an uneasy feeling. I had been to Hell and back... and I had left a part of me in that prison... I wasn't the same AHMAD.
I had a higher calling. I had to join the resistance. I had to tell them about all the moments of fearless chivalry. All the daring and epic events I had witnessed. I wanted to shout, "HEY WORLD!! WE stand so that YOU don't fall!"

CHAPTER 8

THE FINAL FLIGHT

Spring, 1988 – I was growing impatient and decided to act. Wearing a suitable disguise, I went to see my contact. He was a released political prisoner and well-known in the village. I had to approach with caution.

I decided to act and contacted a smuggler who would take me to northwestern Iran- near Urmia. From there, I could join the resistance without being spotted by the Guards. I was unaware that he was an informant!

WHAT THEY DIDN'T KNOW IS THAT IN TIME, A SINGLE SEED CAN GROW INTO A MIGHTY FOREST.

Our hero's story continues....

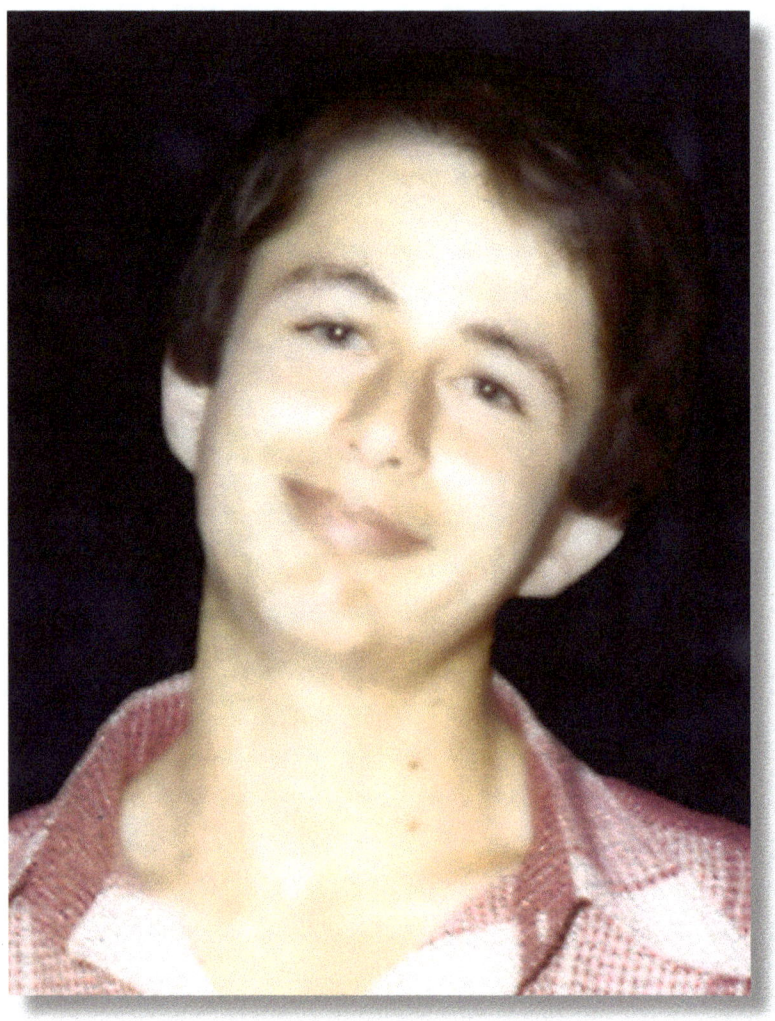

As our hero Ahmad said, they never arrived at Tabriz prison. In August 1988, members of the Islamic Revolutionary Guard Corps (IRGC or Pasdaran) transferred political prisoners to the hills surrounding Lake Urmia.

The prisoners were told that they would be transferred to Tabriz Prison. Agents of the Pasdaran had previously isolated the site of execution in the hills; they were armed with various sharp weapons: machetes, clubs, knives, hatchets and axes.

The prisoners were chained and handcuffed; they were all brutally massacred by the Pasdaran. Villagers who heard the screams of the PMOI prisoners being savagely slain headed for the hills but were arrested and kept away by heavily armed Pasdaran members.

The killing field in the land of the mullahs where the little prince was murdered

Urmia Prison

Western Azerbaijan Province

Location of the mass grave: outskirts of Urmia

Province: Western Azerbaijan

Address: Lake Urmia Hills

Latitude: 37.3507, longitude: 45.0803

Estimated date of burial: August 1988

Notes: Map coordinates are approximate.

Meet all personalities in "A Little Prince in the Land of the Mullahs"

Fatimeh Seighali

Ahmad's mother supported her son to her last breath. She was arrested, imprisoned and tried by a mullah named Moghadassi-Far, a religious judge in the city of Rasht who later became a member of the "Death Committee" of this notable city on the Caspian Sea. The same mullah also sentenced her teenage son, Ahmad, and daughter to long prison terms. Fatimeh's "crime" was to have children active with the opposition group, People's Mojahedin Organization of Iran (PMOI), and her own support for this movement. She died of cancer at the age of 43.

Massoumeh Raouf Basharidoust

Ahmad's sister was arrested in September 1981 and sentenced to 20 years during a 10-minute kangaroo trial. But after eight months she managed to escape. She is currently living in exile. Involved in the Campaign for Justice for the Victims of the 1988 Massacre, she is now advocating to hold the perpetrators accountable for their crimes against humanity.

Hadi Saberi

Ahmad's classmate at Rasht School of Technology; was arrested and tortured by Bassij militia at the Bagherabad Mosque.

He was murdered in 1988. He was 25 years old.

Mohammad-Ali Motamed

A friend and cellmate of Ahmad. He spent 3 years in prison and then joined the Resistance. He was martyred in 1988 at the age of 23.

Rashid Motaghitalab

Ahmad's cellmate at Afsaran Prison in Rasht in 1982. He was murdered in 1988 at the age of 27.

Reza Motaghitalab

Rashid's brother and a supporter of the PMOI at Afsaran Prison in Rasht in 1982. He was murdered in 1988 at the age of 24.

Mohammad-Ali Haghgou

Ahmad's friend and cellmate. After the fire at the Officers Club prison (Afsaran), he managed to escape and joined the Resistance. He lives in exile.

Asghar Mehdizadeh

Ahmad's friend and cellmate. They were incarcerated at Gohardasht prison near the town of Karadj. Asghar who lives in exile is one of the few living witnesses of the massacre of 1988.

The places where our hero lived....

The events in the life of our hero in this book have mainly taken place in Rasht, which is famous for its greenery and a history of resistance against foreign invasion. The capital of Gilan province in northwestern Iran, it is nestled between the Caspian Sea coast and the slopes of the Alborz range on one offshoot of the Sefid-Roud River. The town Rasht was first mentioned in historical documents in 682, but is certainly older. This city has seen the Sassanid period, the armies of Peter the Great (Rasht was where a peace treaty between Persian and Russia was signed in 1732) and later the domination of Russians and the British colonialism.

The district in the city of Rasht where Ahmad lived

Lisar, a beautiful village on the Caspian Sea.

In the first chapter, there is a reference to the history of this region, because the inhabitants of Rasht also played an important role during the Constitutional Revolution of Iran through the Constitutionalist Movement of Gilan. Rasht was the first city proclaimed as a republic in Iran in 1920 by the revolutionaries under the leadership of Mirza Kochek Khan. The movement was violently suppressed by a pro- Russian officer "Reza Khan" who later proclaimed himself king, starting the Pahlavi dynasty.

Mirza Kuchek Khan

"They think we're fools. Our blood in the north comes from a history of resistance!

The School of Technology in Rasht

where Ahmad was a student of electronics. He was tortured by Bassij militiamen at the Bagherabad Mosque.

The dungeons of the IRGC (Pasdaran) in Rasht

The mosque where Ahmad was tortured

1- The Sepah prison in Rasht was the seat of the Pasdaran and a center for interrogation and torture. At the time of the Shah, the building was a large high school for boys before being confiscated by the mullahs. After arrest, prisoners spent their first days and months in the basement of this building, which was converted into a prison.

2- The Revolutionary Court where the show trials were held, and where Ahmad, his sister and his mother were convicted.

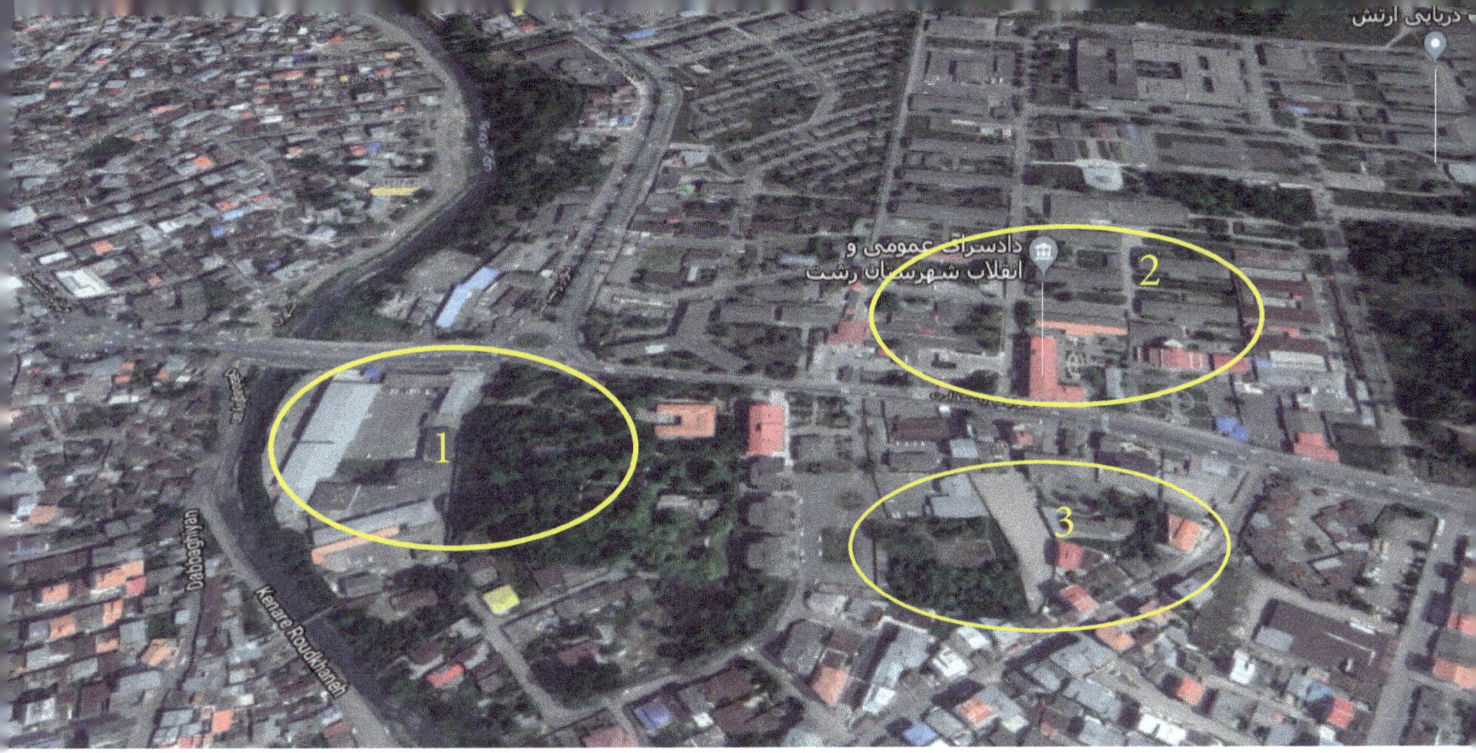

3- Officers' Club Prison (Afsaran): Before the Revolution, the building of this prison housed the Navy Officers' Club often used for parties and weddings. It was confiscated by the Pasdaran who transformed it into a detention center for political prisoners.

Opposite this prison was the "revolutionary" court. The men's section consisted of three rooms and a long corridor.

The layout of Afsaran Prison before the fire

1- Men's section
2- The men's corridor
3- The women's section
4- The cage
5- The torture room and the guards

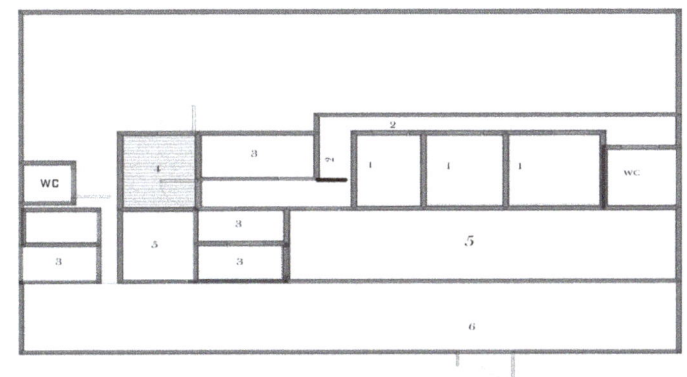

Evin Prison in Tehran

Evin is a large prison complex built during the Shah's regime, located north of Tehran at the foot of the Alborz range that dominates the capital. Khomeini's regime further expanded it, going so far as to transform the administrative part into prison cells. The different sections of Evin prison are controlled by the Ministry of Intelligence and the Revolutionary Guards where they continue to torture and kill political prisoners even to this day.

Geographical coordinates: 35° 47' 43" North, 51° 23' 08" East

Gohardasht Prison in Karaj City

Gohardasht Prison is located in Gohardasht, a district in the northern suburbs of Karaj, about 40 km west of Tehran. It is also called Rajai-Shahr Prison and is infamous for its 1000 cells for solitary confinement. Rajai-Shahr is considered one of the most terrifying prisons in Iran because of the numerous cases of torture, rape and murder that take place there.

The final Flight

According to witnesses, Ahmad's likely route to leave the country was Iran's western borders. He left the city of Rasht and went to Tehran and then to Urmia. He was last seen in Urmia Prison.

Testimony of villagers living in the hills of Lake Urmia

"That night, we heard terrible screams, so we headed for the hills around Lake Urmia. We saw the chained and handcuffed prisoners who were being massacred by white-haired Pasdaran. They were armed with various weapons such as knives, machetes, clubs, axles and axes. The heavily-armed Pasdaran threatened us and moved us away".

The 1988 Massacre in Iran.

August 1988 is a particularly dark month in the annals of the prisons and torture centers of the fundamentalist regime in Iran. A fatwa (religious decree) by Khomeini sparked unprecedented carnage in Iran's contemporary history.

More than 30,000 defenseless political prisoners were put to death within a few months. Most of them had been incarcerated for several years and were waiting to finish their sentences. They were prisoners suffering the after-effects of several years of torture and isolation. Some were brought in with wheelchairs to be hanged.

"Death Commissions" were set up in each city, composed of three members of the regime's security apparatus. Several questions were put to the prisoners, most of whom were waiting to be released in the coming months: Will you condemn your organization? Are you faithful to the Islamic Republic? Will you cooperate?

Although the PMOI members and supporters were the main targets of this systematic killing, all political movements also fell victim to this organized massacre. In prisons across the country, kangaroo courts "tried" prisoners again and sentenced them to death.

More than 30,000 prisoners of conscience were thus exterminated in what can only be described as "a crime against humanity, gone unpunished," whose perpetrators are still in power in Iran.

An international investigation by the UN into this terrible tragedy is expected.

The families of the victims continue their international campaign to shed light on what Amnesty International has described as a "prison massacre."

> **Extracts of the letter by khomeini, declaring the fatwa to massacre**
>
> In the name of Allah, the Compassionate, the Merciful:
>
> As the treacherous Monafeqin [Mojahedin] do not believe in Islam and what they say is out of deception and hypocrisy, and as their leaders have confessed that they have become renegades, and as they are waging war on God, and as they are engaging in classical warfare in the western, northern and southern fronts, and as they are collaborating with the Baathist Party of Iraq and spying for Saddam against our Muslim nation, and as they are tied to the World Arrogance [the US], and in light of their cowardly blows to the Islamic Republic since its inception, it is decreed that those who are in prisons throughout the country and remain steadfast in their support for the Monafeqin [Mojahedin], are waging war on God and are condemned to execution.
>
>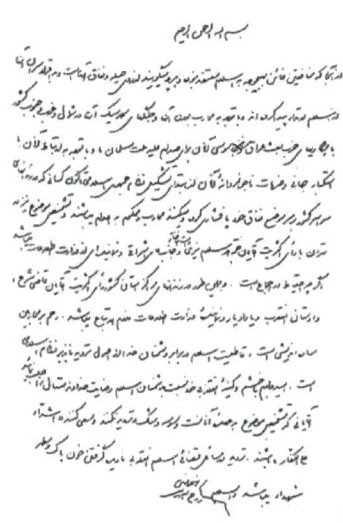
>
> The task of implementing the decree in Tehran is entrusted to Hojjat ol-Islam Nayyeri, the religious judge, Mr. Eshraqi, the Tehran prosecutor, and a representative of the Intelligence Ministry.
>
> Even though a unanimous decision is better, the view of a majority of the three must prevail in prisons in the provinces, the views of a majority of a trio consisting of the religious judge, the revolutionary prosecutor, and the Intelligence Ministry representative must be obeyed. It is naive to show mercy to those who wage war on God. The decisive way in which Islam treats the enemies of God is among the unquestionable tenets of the Islamic regime. I hope that with your revolutionary rage and vengeance toward the enemies of Islam, you will achieve the satisfaction of the Almighty God. Those who are making the decisions must not hesitate, nor show any doubt or be concerned with details. They must try to be "most ferocious against infidels." To doubt the judicial issues in revolutionary Islam is to ignore the pure blood of the martyrs.
>
> Rouhollah Moussavi Khomeini

Who was responsible for the 1988 massacre in Iran?

On the basis of information obtained by the PMOI, the main institutions of the Iranian regime today consist of officials involved in the 1988 massacre of 30,000 political prisoners throughout the country. The PMOI was able to obtain information on 78 individuals responsible for this crime against humanity. Their direct role and identity have been concealed for almost three decades. Members of the "death committee" in Tehran and ten other provinces, they continue to hold key positions in the various institutions of the regime.

What was the "death committee"?

In late July 1988, Khomeini published a fatwa ordering the elimination of political prisoners. Delegations for the implementation of the decree (death committees) were set up in some 70 cities. Previously, only the identities of some members of Tehran's "death committee" were known, having been formally appointed by Khomeini. The death committees were composed of a religious judge, a prosecutor and the representative of the intelligence ministry.

During a meeting in 1988 with members of the death committee in Tehran, the late dissident Ayatollah Hossein-Ali Montazeri, Khomeini's designated successor, denounced the extent of carnage in prisons. Some 30,000 political prisoners, some of them as young as 14 or 15 at the time of their arrests, were eliminated and secretly buried in mass graves.

In a document published by the PMOI listing the victims of the Iranian regime during the 1988 massacre, 789 adolescents, 62 pregnant women, and 410 families with more than three members executed can be noted. However, this is only a partial list drawn up under conditions of underground activity.

3 questions determining Life or Death!

Judge: "Your political affiliation, are you a hypocrite?"
Prisoner: No

Judge: "Are you ready to condemn the hypocrites? "
Prisoner: No

Judge: "Are you ready to do a TV (confession) interview? "
Prisoner: No

Judge: "So you are a traitor. …next (for execution).

Allahverdi Moghadassi-far,

Moghaddassi-far was the religious judge of the city of Rasht, who convicted Ahmad, his sister and his mother.
Later on, during the 1988 massacre, he was a principal member of the provincial "death committee".
He signed the death warrant for thousands of young opponents.
He is currently the Vice-President for Legal Affairs and Deputy President of the Administrative Court of Justice.

United Nations

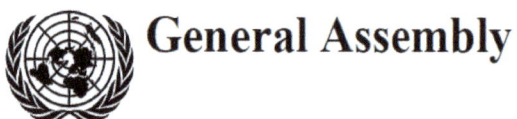

General Assembly

A/HRC/38/NGO/122

Distr.: General
13 June 2018

High Commissioner should bring his support to the International Commission of Inquiry into the 1988 massacres in Iran.

Human Rights Council - Thirty-eighth Session
18 June-6 July 2018

Joint written statement submitted by the International Association of Women and Human Rights, France-Libertés (Danielle Mitterand Foundation, non-governmental organizations in special consultative status), Mouvement contre le racisme et pour l'amitié entre les peoples (MRAP), non-governmental organization on the list.

A major factor behind the Iranian authorities' cynicism in continuing to eliminate opponents today is the impunity they enjoy over earlier human rights atrocities, the most horrific of which was the massacre of 30,000 political prisoners in 1988.

These executions were carried out following a decree issued by the Supreme Leader, Ayatollah Khomeini. This decree ordered the execution of all political prisoners affiliated to the People's Mojahedin Organization of Iran (PMOI or MEK), the main opposition group, who remained loyal to this organization. Committees of three members, known as "death committees", were formed throughout the Iranian territory and executed political prisoners who refused to renounce their political convictions.

Political prisoners from other resistance groups were executed in a second wave of repression about one month after the killings began. All the victims were buried in secret mass graves.

Their perpetrators continue to enjoy total impunity. Many of them hold senior positions in the Iranian judicial system or in government. The current Minister of Justice is one of them...

Almost 30 years after the extra-judicial mass executions of political prisoners in Iran, we believe that until the full truth is revealed and the perpetrators are held fully accountable, the Iranian government will have no reason to change its current human rights policy.

Report of the UN Special Rapporteur

on the situation of human rights in the Islamic Republic of Iran on 5 March 2018 (Extract)

Summary executions in 1988

.... 21. Since the publication of her previous report, the Special Rapporteur has continued to receive documents and letters concerning the summary execution and enforced disappearance of thousands of political prisoners, men, women and adolescents in 1988. More than 150 individual applications were received during 2017. The Special Rapporteur also met with the families of some of the victims during her missions. They described the difficulties they had encountered in obtaining information on these events, known as the 1988 massacres, which continue to be officially not recognized. The Special Rapporteur has also heard first-hand testimony on the harassment of those who continue to request additional information on the events of 1988.

22. The Special Rapporteur reiterates that families have the right to recourse, reparation and the right to know the truth about the 1988 massacres and the fate of the victims.

The Special Rapporteur is also concerned about reports of desecration of mass graves in Mashhad city, Khorassan Razavi province and Ahvaz, and urges the Government to ensure that all sites are preserved and protected until investigations into the events can be conducted.

Ayatollah Ali Montazeri:

"The greatest crime committed during the Islamic Republic, for which history will condemn us, has been committed by you."

In the summer of 2016, the shocking broadcast of an audio tape recording in the social media shed light on the magnitude of this 1988 massacre. This recording was made public after 28 years and was a real shock to the Iranian people.

It was an audio tape of secret meeting held on August 15, 1988, between Ayatollah Ali Montazeri, successor of Khomeini (at the time), and members of the "commission of death", responsible for carrying out Khomeini's decree of mass executions.

In this recording, Montazeri distinctively said: "The biggest crime committed under the Islamic Republic, for which history will condemn us, was committed by you. Your (names) will be engraved in the annals of history as those of criminals."

Montazeri was dismissed by Khomeini and died in 2009 while under house arrest.

Anzali (nord)

Soume'eh Sara

Tabriz (nord-ouest)

Ahwaz (sud-ouest)

Dezfoul (sud-ouest)

Racht (nord)

Andimechk (sud-ouest)

Bandar-Abbas (su…

"Justice for Iran":
There are more than 120 identified mass graves of victims of the 1988 massacre across Iran.

Amnesty 30 April 2018, (excerpt)

New evidence, including analysis of satellite imagery, photos and videos, shows that Iranian authorities are deliberately destroying suspected or known sites of mass graves linked to the 1988 massacre, during which thousands of politically-motivated prisoners were subjected to enforced disappearance and extra-judicially executed, according to a report published on 30 April by Amnesty International and Justice for Iran.

This report, entitled "Criminal Cover-up: Iran Destroying Mass Graves of Victims of 1988 Killings", reveals that Iranian authorities are carrying out earthworks, constructing buildings and roads, depositing garbage and establishing new burial concessions at mass grave sites.

"The atrocities committed in Iran during the 1988 massacre opened a wound that never closed. By destroying this crucial forensic evidence, the Iranian authorities are deliberately reinforcing a climate of impunity," said Philip Luther, Director of Research and Advocacy for Amnesty International's North Africa and Middle East Programme.

"These are crime scenes that must be protected as such until independent and meaningful forensic investigations are conducted to identify the remains of the victims and determine the circumstances of their deaths," said Shadi Sadr, Director of Justice for Iran.

Ispahan (centre)

Arak (centre)

Téhéran

Gorgan (nord)

Téhéran

Téhéran – Cimetière de Behecht-Zahra

For nearly 30 years, the Iranian authorities have persistently concealed the fate of the victims and have not revealed where their bodies are. These are enforced disappearances, a practice that constitutes a crime under international law.

"It has been thirty years since this merciless massacre took place; it is high time the authorities took real steps to reveal, not hide, the truth. You can't just erase the memory of the people who were killed, or bury it under a concrete slab," Luther said.

Photos

1- Anzali (north) - Mass graves of victims of the 1988 massacre
2- Soume'eh Sara / Kasma (North) - Victims are buried in this orchard.
3- Tabriz (northwest) - Vadi Rahmat Cemetery
4- Ahwaz (south-west), Behecht-Abad cemetery - The regime wanted to cover the graves by drowning them in water.
5- Isfahan (center) - Mass graves.
6- Arak (center) - The Aramestan cemetery contains mass graves.
7- Tehran - Khavaran Cemetery, main site of mass graves of victims of the 1988 massacre.
8- Dezfoul (south-west) - Mass graves on which buildings of the "sacred defense center" were built.
9- Racht (north) - Tazeh-Abad Cemetery.
10- Andimechk (south-west) - Mass graves on which a park was built.
11- Bandar-Abbas (south) - Mass graves.
12- Gorgan (north) - Jangali Park where a large number of victims are buried.
13- Tehran - Cemetery of Behecht-Zahra. Section 41. Mass graves are scattered in various sections, including Nos. 287, 105, 106, 99, 98, 93 and 41.

Who are the People's Mojahedin Organization of Iran (PMOI)?

The People's Mojahedin Organization of Iran (PMOI or MEK) is a pro-democracy Muslim movement that has become the main opposition to the Khomeini regime. The organization was founded in 1965 by intellectuals who supported the democratic prime minister, Mohammad Mossadegh, as the champion of secular democracy and resistance to foreign domination in Iran's modern history, who had nationalized the Iranian oil industry in 1950. Advocating a tolerant and democratic Islam, they opposed the Shah's dictatorship that executed the PMOI founders and many other members. After the 1979 revolution, they became widely popular among Iranian youth, emerging as the first political force of opposition to the mullahs' dictatorship.

The People's Mojahedin refused to endorse the Constitution of the theocratic government and the principle of a Supreme Leader as guardian of the people. This refusal resulted in their very harsh repression. More than 120,000 of their members and supporters have been executed by this regime. On June 20, 1981, Khomeini ordered the massacre of a large peaceful demonstration of 500,000 PMOI supporters in Tehran, putting an end to any possibility of legal opposition. The organization then began a long-lasting resistance against the theocratic regime. In July 1981, Massoud Rajavi, the leader of the PMOI, founded the coalition of the National Council of Resistance of Iran (NCRI) in Tehran, which advocates the establishment of a secular and pluralist republic, equality of women and men and respect for human rights.

Massoud Rajavi, leader of the People's Mojahedin in 1979

Ahmad Raouf Basharidoust
A soul stolen in the 1988 massacre

Ahmad was only 16 years old in 1982, when he was arrested at his home in a raid by the Revolutionary Guards (Pasdaran) in Rasht. Previously, he had been arrested a number of times between 1980 to 1981 for opposing the Mullahs. Each time, he was tortured for having participated in meetings of the People's Mojahedin Organization of Iran (PMOI), the democratic opposition to the mullahs.

In late 1982, after several rounds of interrogation and torture, Ahmad was sentenced to five years in prison by a mullah named Moghadassi-Far, a religious judge in the town of Rasht. On March 12, 1983, the Pasdaran set the Afsaran Prison on fire and killed several political prisoners who tried to escape the flames. Seven prisoners affiliated with the PMOI perished in that fire. Ahmad who lost consciousness was rescued by a fellow prisoner.

But a few months later, in June 1983, Rasht's prosecutor, unable to break the resistance in the prison, decided to exile forty prisoners including Ahmad. He was transferred to Evin in Tehran, then to Gohardasht Prison in Karaj. "In 1984 I finally got a very short visit. Ahmad had signs of torture and beatings. He told me very quickly what had happened and how they had tortured him during the month of Ramadan while he was fasting. Ahmad asked me to report their heroic strike to the People's Mojahedin Organization", Ahmad's relative tells us. They had gone on hunger strike to protest the inhuman conditions in prison and the savagery of the regime.

Ahmad was released after almost 6 years in prison in March 1988 and was seeking to leave the country to join the exiled Resistance.

In March 1988, he wrote to his sister in exile about the conditions of his detention "If I wanted to tell you what I lived through during these years, I could write volumes, so

let us leave the account of this forced journey and these pains endured for another time."

But a couple of months later he fell into an intelligence ministry trap and was arrested for the last time and taken away under torture. This time he was imprisoned in the city of Urmia, in northwest of Iran.

In August 1988, members of the Pasdaran transported political prisoners, mostly PMOI members, including Ahmad, to the hills surrounding Lake Urmia using two minibuses. The prisoners were told that they would be transferred to another prison in Tabriz. Agents of the Pasdaran had previously prepared a secluded site for execution on the hills. They were armed with various sharp blades including machetes, clubs, knives, hatchets and axes.

The prisoners were chained and handcuffed; they were brutally massacred by the Pasdaran. Villagers who heard the screams of the PMOI prisoners being savagely slain headed for the hills but were arrested and kept away by heavily armed Pasdaran members.

Ahmad and his mother in 1981

In 1991, in search of Ahmad's whereabout, his father was informed by regime's intelligence agents to sop looking for him as he was already executed in Urmia. To this day, the regime has not revealed where they have buried Ahmad remains.

In prison, he wrote poems:

Overwhelmed by misfortune, Iran is not silenced,
In our long night, the blood of the innocent flows everywhere.
Thanks to our fight, however tomorrow the sun will rise,
We mustn't sleep. We must act.
We must swear an oath in the name of the blood of the innocent,

We must act.   We must act.

"THE TRUTH IS ON THE MARCH AND NOTHING WILL STOP IT."

*"When truth is buried underground it grows,
it chokes, it gathers such an explosive force
that on the day it bursts out,
it blows up everything with it."*

Émile Zola

You can share Ahmad's story in social media;

to leave a comment please visit:

 iran.petitprince@gmail.com

 @AhmadRaouf1343

http://iran-petit-prince.blogspot.com

List of Publications

List of Publications by the National Council of Resistance of Iran, U.S. Representative Office

Iran's Emissaries of Terror

June 2019, 208 pages

This book explains the extent to which Tehran's embassies and diplomats are at the core of both the planning and execution of international terrorism targeting Iranian dissidents, as well as central to Tehran's direct and proxy terrorism against other countries.

Iran Doubles Down on Terror and Turmoil

November 2018, 63 pages

This book examines the regime's political and economic strategy, which revolves around terrorism and physical annihilation of opponents. Failing to quell growing popular protests, Tehran has bolstered domestic suppression with blatant terrorism and intimidation.

Iran Will Be Free:
Speech by Maryam Rajavi

September 2018, 54 pages

This manuscript contains delivered keynote speech by Mrs. Maryam Rajavi, on June 30, 2018, at the Iranian Resistance's grand gathering in Paris, France explaining the path to freedom in Iran and what she envisions for future Iran.

Iran's Ballistic Buildup: The March Toward Nuclear-Capable Missiles
May 2018, 136 pages

This manuscript surveys Iran's missile capabilities, including the underlying organization, structure, production, and development infrastructure, as well as launch facilities and the command centers. The book exposes the nexus between the regime's missile activities and its nuclear weapons program, including ties with North Korea.

Iran: Cyber Repression: How the IRGC Uses Cyberwarfare to Preserve the Theocracy
February 2018, 70 pages

This manuscript demonstrates how the Iranian regime, under the supervision and guidance of the IRGC and the Ministry of Intelligence and Security (MOIS), have employed new cyberwarfare and tactics in a desperate attempt to counter the growing dissent inside the country.

Iran: Where Mass Murderers Rule: The 1988 Massacre of 30,000 Political Prisoners and the Continuing Atrocities
November 2017, 161 pages

Iran: Where Mass Murderers Rule is an expose of the current rulers of Iran and their track record in human rights violations. The book details how 30,000 political prisoners fell victim to politicide during the summer of 1988 and showcases the egregious political extinction of a group of people.

Iran's Nuclear Core: Uninspected Military Sites, Vital to the Nuclear Weapons Program
October 2017, 52 pages

This book details how the nuclear weapons program is at the heart of, and not parallel to, the civil nuclear program of Iran. The program has been run by the Islamic Revolutionary Guards Corp (IRGC) since the beginning, and the main nuclear sites and nuclear research facilities have been hidden from the eyes of the United Nations nuclear watchdog.

Terrorist Training Camps in Iran: How Islamic Revolutionary Guards Corps Trains Foreign Fighters to Export Terrorism

June 2017, 56 pages

The book details how Islamic Revolutionary Guards Corps trains foreign fighters in 15 various camps in Iran to export terrorism. The IRGC has created a large directorate within its extraterritorial arm, the Quds Force, in order to expand its training of foreign mercenaries as part of the strategy to step up its meddling abroad in Syria, Iraq, Yemen, Bahrain, Afghanistan and elsewhere.

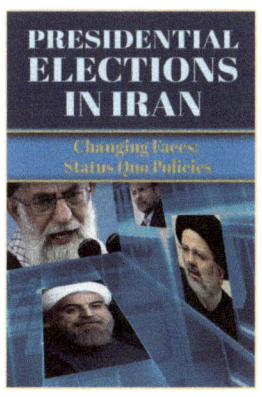

Presidential Elections in Iran: Changing Faces; Status Quo Policies

May 2017, 78 pages

The book reviews the past 11 presidential elections, demonstrating that the only criterion for qualifying as a candidate is practical and heartfelt allegiance to the Supreme Leader. An unelected vetting watchdog, the Guardian Council makes that determination.

The Rise of Iran's Revolutionary Guards' Financial Empire: How the Supreme Leader and the IRGC Rob the People to Fund International Terror

March 2017, 174 pages

This study shows how ownership of property in various spheres of the economy is gradually shifted from the population writ large towards a minority ruling elite comprised of the Supreme Leader's office and the IRGC, using 14 powerhouses, and how the money ends up funding terrorism worldwide.

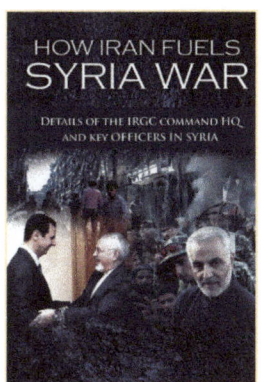

How Iran Fuels Syria War: Details of the IRGC Command HQ and Key Officers in Syria

November 2016, 74 pages

This book examines how the Iranian regime has effectively engaged in the military occupation of Syria by marshaling 70,000 forces, including the Islamic Revolutionary Guard Corps (IRGC) and mercenaries from other countries into Syria; is paying monthly salaries to over 250,000 militias and agents to prolong the conflict; and divided the country into 5 zones of conflict, establishing 18 command, logistics and operations centers.

Nowruz 2016 with the Iranian Resistance: Hoping for a New Day, Freedom and Democracy in Iran

April 2016, 36 pages

This book describes Iranian New Year, Nowruz celebrations at the Washington office of Iran's parliament-in-exile, the National Council of Resistance of Iran. The yearly event marks the beginning of spring. It includes select speeches by dignitaries who have attended the NCRIUS Nowruz celebrations.

The 2016 Vote in Iran's Theocracy: An analysis of Parliamentary & Assembly of Experts Elections

February 2016, 70 pages

This book examines all the relevant data about the 2016 Assembly of Experts as well as Parliamentary elections ahead of the February 2016 elections. It looks at the history of elections since the revolution in 1979 and highlights the current intensified infighting among the various factions of the Iranian regime.

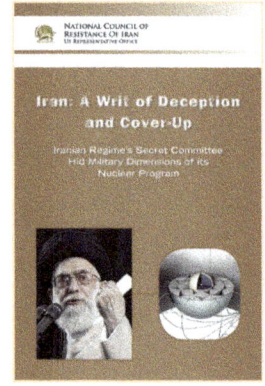

IRAN: A Writ of Deception and Cover-up: Iranian Regime's Secret Committee Hid Military Dimensions of its Nuclear Program

February 2016, 30 pages

The book provides details about a top-secret committee in charge of forging response to the International Atomic Energy Agency (IAEA) regarding the Possible Military Dimensions (PMD) of Tehran's nuclear program, including those related to the detonators called EBW (Exploding Bridge Wire), an integral part of developing an implosion type nuclear device.

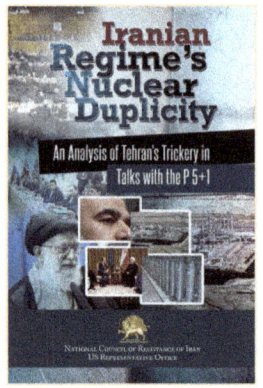

Iranian Regime's Nuclear Duplicity: An Analysis of Tehran's Trickery in Talks with the P 5+1

January 2016, 74 pages

This book examines Iran's behavior throughout the negotiations process in an effort to inform the current dialogue on a potential agreement. Drawing on both publicly available sources and those within Iran, the book focuses on two major periods of intense negotiations with the regime: 2003-2004 and 2013-2015.

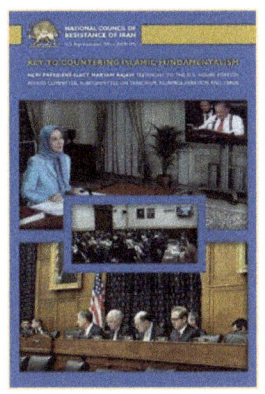

Key to Countering Islamic Fundamentalism: Maryam Rajavi? Testimony To The U.S. House Foreign Affairs Committee

June 2015, 68 pages

Testimony before U.S. House Foreign Affairs Committee's subcommittee on Terrorism, non-Proliferation, and Trade discussing ISIS and Islamic fundamentalism. The book contains Maryam Rajavi's full testimony as well as the question and answer by representatives.

Meet the National Council of Resistance of Iran

June 2014, 150 pages

Meet the National Council of Resistance of Iran discusses what NCRI stands for, what its platform is, and why a vision for a free, democratic, secular, non-nuclear republic in Iran would serve world peace.

How Iran Regime Cheated the World: Tehran's Systematic Efforts to Cover Up its Nuclear Weapons Program

June 2014, 50 pages

The monograph discusses the Iranian regime's report card as far as it relates to being transparent when addressing the international community's concerns about the true nature and the ultimate purpose of its nuclear program.

About the NCRI-US

The National Council of Resistance of Iran-US Representative Office (NCRI-US) acts as the Washington office for Iran's parliament-in-exile, the National Council of Resistance of Iran, which is dedicated to the establishment of a democratic, secular, non-nuclear republic in Iran.

NCRI-US, registered as a non-profit tax-exempt organization, has been instrumental in exposing the nuclear weapons program of Iran, including the sites in Natanz, and Arak, the biological and chemical weapons program of Iran, as well as its ambitious ballistic missile program.

NCRI-US has also exposed the terrorist network of the regime, including its involvement in the bombing of Khobar Towers in Saudi Arabia, the Jewish Community Center in Argentina, its fueling of sectarian violence in Iraq and Syria, and its malign activities in other parts of the Middle East.

Our office has provided information on the human rights violations in Iran, extensive anti-government demonstrations, and the movement for democratic change in Iran.

Visit our website at www.ncrius.org

You may follow us on	twitter	@ncrius
Follow us on	facebook	NCRIUS
You can also find us on	Instagram	NCRIUS

www.ingramcontent.com/pod-product-compliance
Lightning Source LLC
Chambersburg PA
CBHW041646040426
R18086900001B/R180869PG42333CBX00020B/3